MORE OF
ABING

PAST & PRESENT

Judy Thomas
&
Elizabeth Drury

An MG sports car enters the town over Abingdon Bridge in 1996. European towns twinned with the Vale of White Horse District Council and Abingdon Town Council are featured on the sign.

Saint Helen Publishing
33 East Saint Helen Street
Abingdon
Oxfordshire
OX14 5EE

First published 2008

Copyright:
© Judy Thomas & Elizabeth Drury, 2008

ISBN 978-0-9560466-1-1

Design: Organ Graphic Design
design@organgraphic.com

Cover photographs

Front: MG cars leave the Morland Brewery site in
Ock Street at the start of an MG rally in 1997.

Back: Morland's employees pose in Morland's yard in
Ock Street with their decorated waggons for the
celebration of Queen Victoria's Diamond Jubilee in
1897. The covered waggon on the right is the one
used for the celebration of Queen Victoria's accession
in 1837, with the draymen dressed in 'period'
costume. The house in the background is Ock Lea,
the residence of the Morland family in 1861.

The annual Michaelmas Fair in Ock Street in the 1920s.

Contents

Children from Dunmore Primary School wait in Park Road for the arrival of Queen Elizabeth II on her visit to Abingdon in 1956 for the 400th anniversary of the granting of Abingdon's Borough Charter in 1556.

Introduction

The photographs in the first 'Abingdon Past & Present' book documented the changing scene in the town centre. This second volume records changes in the wider town, including the River Thames, Ock Street, Albert Park and outlying areas. But the changes in the town's appearance reflect more fundamental changes in the character of Abingdon itself over the past sixty years.

When World War II ended in 1945 Abingdon was much as it had been for the previous 300 years – a typical market town of under 10,000 inhabitants, somewhat run down but with a sense of its own importance due to its long and illustrious history. For nearly 900 years the great Benedictine Abbey of St Mary had dominated the life of the town. The dissolution of the Abbey in 1538 was a serious blow, but with the granting of its Borough Charter in 1556 Abingdon became the County Town of Berkshire, a position which it held until 1869.

From early times – possibly even in the Roman period – Abingdon was a market town serving the surrounding villages and closely connected to the countryside. Many of its inhabitants were involved with agriculture in one way or another and there were many shops supplying farmers' needs, such as animal feedstuffs, harness and farm machinery. Local farms supplied the butchers, grocers, greengrocers and fruiterers with their produce; malthouses and breweries used barley from nearby farms; animal hides were processed in the town's leather factories and there were numerous nursery gardens. The Ock Fair, which is still the town's most important fair, was formerly a hiring fair where farm workers, milkmaids and servant girls would seek employment for the following year.

Like many English country towns, Abingdon also had a strong industrial base. By 1945 its industries included the MG car works, Morland brewery, three leather factories and several printing works. It was also a perfect illustration of the old saying that Britain was a nation of shopkeepers. Its shops sold goods of every description from hats to hardware, sweets to shoes and clothing to carpets. Many of these commodities were made on the premises, in small workshops or at home. Coxeter's manufactured a light motor-cycle, the 'Abingdon Cycle' in 1900 and there was even an 'Abingdon Car' long before the famous MG car factory moved from Oxford to Abingdon in 1929.

The Victorian period had brought a population explosion, from 4,683 in 1801 to 6,848 in 1851, but the town had not expanded so overcrowding was rife. Nowhere is this better illustrated than in Ock Street which was notorious for its crowded 'courts' of tiny houses running back from the street frontage, as well as rows of tall brick town houses such as 'Pig Row', which was replaced by a modern housing block in the 1960s. A high percentage of the town's industries were located in Ock Street and some of these still survive, but none of the many small food shops remain apart from restaurants and take-aways.

The Borough Council had initiated a programme of slum clearance in the 1930s when residents of the old 'courts' in the town centre were moved to new council housing on Saxton Road to the south of the town. This continued after the war with more council estates in south Abingdon and in the Fitzharry's area. The creation of AERE Harwell and the Rutherford and Culham Laboratories in the 1950s brought an influx of scientists to live in new Harwell estates on Fitzharry's and Appleford Drive. The demolition of Fitzharry's Manor in 1953 was followed by Barton Court in 1967, Caldecott House in 1972 and The Warren in 1982. Today even quite modest houses with large gardens are under threat for their development potential.

Sailing boats on a tranquil summer's day
above Abingdon lock, before the present weir
and gangway were constructed in the 1960s.

Housing estates have also engulfed most of the farms which used to surround Abingdon. Dunmore, Barton, Ladygrove, Tithe Farm, Corporation Farm, Northcourt and part of Peachcroft which once provided milk, eggs, beef, lamb, fruit and vegetables for local consumption have all been built over. Only Peachcroft (see Chapter 8) still has enough land to be a viable farm. Abingdon's role as a market town diminished when the cattle market closed in 1988, although there is still a Monday market, supplemented by a monthly Farmers' Market and more recently, a French Market. The loss of the livestock market reflected wider changes in food production and distribution. This book records some of Abingdon's lost agricultural heritage as well as changes in the town itself.

House building and gravel digging have been just two of the pressures driving development. The need for new roads to cope with ever-increasing traffic has combined with far-reaching changes in the patterns of work and trade. Roads such as Stratton Way have affected the old street patterns. There has been a policy of removing industries such as garages and car repair workshops from the town centre to industrial sites. The A34 by-pass and the inner relief road have facilitated the relocation of large businesses such as May's Carpets (now Carpetright) and Viney's furniture store to out-of-town retail parks, and the arrival of Tesco's store has had a considerable impact on the town and on people's shopping habits.

The following paragraph, written by Abingdon Corporation in 1970 *, perfectly sums up these changes:

"Those who did not know Abingdon in the Forties cannot realise just how much it has grown in the Fifties and Sixties. When the Second World War ended Fitzharry's Manor and Fitzharris [sic]Farm still existed; Northcourt still had something of the character of a separate village; Rush Common really was a piece of grazing land, and Saxton Road set an unbroken, monotonous limit to the southward expansion of the town. The Abbey Meadow was private farmland, and as towing had died out the public only enjoyed a tenuous and uncertain privilege of walking along the Oxfordshire bank entirely at the discretion of the landowner. Only the Abingdon Town Football Club had gained a real foothold on the water meadows."

The growth of the town has been even more dramatic since Abingdon became part of the Vale of White Horse in Oxfordshire in 1974, following local government reorganisation. Abingdon is now the headquarters of the District Council and is still the most important town in the Vale, but the Town Council now has more limited powers.

The population has increased from under 10,000 in 1945 to over 33,000 today. Many people commute to work in Oxford, London and elsewhere. Traditional industries such as the MG Car Company, Henry Booth and the Pavlova Leather Company, Morland's Brewery and Burgess the printers have been bought out and their sites sold for housing. They have been replaced by modern businesses such as Sophos, Oxford Instruments and Oxford Genome Sciences, on out-of-town sites.

Fortunately the town's riverside setting remains largely unspoiled. Abingdonians can still enjoy the pleasures of the recreation area in the Abbey Meadow, or a stroll by the river. Salter's steamers still run twice-daily trips to and from Oxford in the summer, and boating is still a popular pastime. Although much else has changed, Abingdon remains a lively, important place, but very different from the Abingdon of former times as these photographs demonstrate.

Judy Thomas

2008

*An extract from the introduction to the *Road to the Seventies – Two Decades of Achievement in Abingdon and District* reproduced by kind permission of Abingdon Town Council.

1
Approaching Abingdon – the Causeway, Bridge and River

Abingdon from the Causeway, c.1909. The low hedges allow a clear view of the bridges and the Nag's Head pub across the fields. The Causeway was built at the same time as Abingdon and Culham bridges in 1416 because of frequent flooding.

Abingdon from the Causeway.

THE CAUSEWAY, ABINGDON.

Four children pose on the deserted Causeway in this wintry picture of c.1910. The bare trees are in striking contrast to the leafy scene in the previous picture.

Nowadays the Causeway is busy with traffic, and the overgrown hedgerow hides the view of the town. Only the spire of St. Helen's church is visible above the trees.

The run-down buildings of Rye Farm on Andersey Island in 1991. William I had a hunting lodge on Andersey in the 11th century, but the Abbot of Abingdon Abbey found the noise of the hounds so disturbing that he persuaded the king to exchange Andersey for land in Sutton Courtenay.

In the early 1990s the farm buildings were converted into what is now the Kingfisher Barns holiday centre. The dilapidated barn (above right) has been demolished.

The River Thames below Abingdon Bridge, c. 1910. The construction of the Abingdon and Culham bridges and the Causeway in 1416 made a more direct route from London to the west country and brought great prosperity to the town. Mr C A Pryce, a local solicitor, presented the fishing rights of the Thames to the Council in 1895, 'for the free enjoyment of the public'.

The bridge was first widened in 1820. A further major reconstruction took place in 1929 when the old navigation arch was replaced by this graceful arch. The Nag's Head pub now occupies both buildings on the bridge.

The overgrown islands by Abingdon Bridge, c.1910. The notice on Nag's Head Island advertises 'good camping ground'. The Abingdon Carpet Factory, one of the town's important industries, can be seen (left background). The factory went out of business in the 1930s, partly as result of cheap German imports at that time.

Motor cruisers are moored alongside the landing stage on Nag's Head Island, where shrubs and flowerbeds now create a colourful welcome.

This 1918 photograph shows the removal of an island which lay alongside Nag's Head Island (upper right) just below Abingdon Bridge. Several barges and a tug are visible in the channel between the two islands. The plant cover has been stripped away and the soil is being loaded onto the waiting barges. The land on the south bank of the river was privately owned and, apart from the towpath, was fenced off at this date.

Day cruisers are moored beside the modern boat station on Nag's Head Island. In 1928 the Master and Governors of Christ's Hospital offered to let the wooded area known as the 'Rookery' (upper left) to the Corporation for a children's playground at five shillings per annum. Now all the land on the south bank of the river is available for the public to enjoy.

The entrance to Nag's Head Island from Abingdon bridge, c.1918. A rowing boat sits on trestles (left) while a pony stands behind the gate. As well as grazing for cows and horses, the island also had allotments and was used by local boys for camping in summer.

The island has been transformed to cater for the leisure trade. Here the row of small boats seen on the opposite page has been laid up for the winter.

A young family enjoy the riverside walk in 1963. The Malthouse (left) and Fairlawn Wharf (right) were once a hive of activity. The Malthouse, which became a private house in 1900, was the centre of the Abingdon malt trade in the 18th century. The wharf was used to bring in coal, iron and other commodities such as hides for the Pavlova Leather Factory in Cemetery Road.

Pleasure cruisers are moored along the piled and concreted river bank opposite Fairlawn Wharf. A proposal to demolish the old warehouses and replace them with 'Costa Brava' style flats in 1972 caused a public outcry. The scheme was rejected and the warehouses were converted into riverside residences.

2
The Abbey, River and Lock

Generations of Abingdonians have enjoyed the quiet pleasures of the town's riverside setting, seen here in the 1930s. The new navigation arch of the bridge is visible to the left of Nag's Head Island, with its tea gardens and landing stage for Salter's steamers. The large building on the right is the Abingdon Carpet factory.

THE RIVER AND TEA GARDENS, ABINGDON.

The car repair workshop and old cottage at 10 and 11 Abbey Close in 1973, with October House beyond.

Abbey Close today. In the mid 1970s the workshop was replaced by these brick buildings belonging to the Strict Baptist Mission. The cobbled pavement has recently been resurfaced. The abbey church and monastic buildings, including the cloisters, refectory and dormitory, stood behind the stone wall on the left.

The derelict Abbey Buildings in 1938, with the 'Granatory or Garner' (centre), the bakehouse (right) and the famous Checker chimney (left). The bakehouse was used as a prison and gaoler's house for many years and the Granatory had been converted into four cottages. One of these was occupied by old Mrs Williams who made and sold boiled sweets.

The 'Friends of Abingdon' Civic Society was formed in 1944 to protect the town's heritage. They saved the Abbey Buildings from demolition and gradually restored them. The Granatory is now the popular Unicorn Theatre and the bakehouse is the Curator's house and Friends' office, pictured here with the late Curator, Peter Berrell and his wife Jenny, who is the present Curator.

Above. A 19th century engraving of the 13th century Checker building of Abingdon Abbey, viewed from inside the barn opposite (see p.19) where a cart-horse is feeding from a trough. It was then part of the Abbey Brewery and the undercroft below the wooden balustrade was being used to store beer barrels.

Above right. The Checker building in 1875 with the staircase to the upper room still in place. The buildings were purchased and restored by the Borough Council in 1895.

Right. A new free-standing staircase gives access once again to the upper room of the Checker. The doorway on the left leads into the vaulted undercroft, formerly the Abbot's wine cellar.

Cottages, barns and stables once filled the yard opposite the Long Gallery.

Surrounded by neat paths, flowers and shrubs, these attractive buildings are a small remnant of Abingdon's once-great Abbey. Opaque blinds now shield the open Long Gallery from the worst of the weather, enabling it to be used for many functions.

The creeper-covered gardener's cottage beside the mill-stream opposite the Coserner's House. The cottage is believed to have been one of the Abbey's fulling mills for whitening the woollen cloth for which the Abbey was famous. The half-timbered gateway (far right) led into a stable yard.

The cottage was converted into a house for visiting scientists in 1970 and the stables have also been converted into guest accommodation. The present Coserner's House, now a guest house and conference centre for the Rutherford Appleton Laboratory, is on the site once occupied by the abbey Kitchener, or Cuisinier, hence the name.

Abbey House and Gardens, Abingdon

A postcard view of Abbey House with its formal gardens, once the home of the Bishop of Reading. The Bishop moved from Abingdon in 1921 and the house with its 16 acres of grounds was bought by Abingdon Corporation in 1923 for £5,500.

The house and formal gardens are little changed, but they are now overlooked by the new District Council offices, also called Abbey House, built in 1991. 'Old Abbey House' is now the headquarters of Abingdon Town Council.

The ivy-clad folly in the grounds of Abbey House in its Victorian heyday. A stone balustrade, ornamental urns and lush planting create an exotic effect. The gardens were created by Mr E J Trendell who was Mayor of Abingdon in 1858 and 1859. He lived in Abbey House from 1853 until his death in 1900.

The delicate tracery has disappeared and the surviving stonework, stripped of ivy, has recently been restored. Frequently mistaken for part of Abingdon Abbey, some of the stonework came from the west window of St. Helen's Church during the 1873 restoration. The curious stone in the foreground is said to contain a cannon ball from the English Civil War.

The ornamental lake and island in the gardens of Abbey House, part of the Victorian pleasure gardens created by the owner, Mr E J Trendell, in the mid 1800s. An elaborate rockery, stone balustrade and summer house add an air of romance.

This children's playground, shaded by tall trees, was for many years a popular feature of the Abbey Grounds.

The playground has been resited in the Abbey meadow nearby, and the overgrown pond and island have been dredged and replanted as part of a million-pound project to restore the Abbey Grounds, funded by the Heritage Lottery Fund and the Vale of White Horse District Council and completed in 2007.

A row of young poplar trees shelters the newly-created paddling pool in Abbey meadow, c.1967. There was formerly a paddling pool in the Abbey Grounds.

Here children are enjoying the paddling pool in 2000. The riverside recreation area is a popular place for relaxation on warm summer days. As well as an outdoor swimming pool there are tennis courts, crazy golf and a pitch and putt course.

The paddling pool has been replaced by a modern water feature and the fully-grown poplars screen a large, new children's playground.

Passengers on Salter's steamer, the 'Wargrave', enjoy the tranquil sight of fishermen and swimmers in 1935. The public bathing place (far right) was on an island below the weir. Swimmers were ferried over in a large punt by the manager, Mr Owen. A newspaper article of 1889 claimed that when the Swimming Club opened in 1881, only two members could swim, but it had turned out over 100 good swimmers since then.

The open-air swimming pool in Abbey meadow in 1996. The slide and mats were popular features. The pool was threatened with closure in 1995, and again in 2005 due to lack of money, but spirited campaigns have saved this popular community asset.

Main picture: This 1930s painting by local artist Oswald Couldrey vividly captures a lively session at the bathing place on the island.

A solitary figure stands on the deserted bathing place in the late afternoon sun in 1914. The lock and weir can be seen in the background, as in the Couldrey picture.

Bathing Place, Abingdon.

The island which housed the bathing place is now overgrown and deserted, and swimming in the river is not encouraged.

A steamer passes through Abingdon Lock, c.1900. The lock-keeper and his assistant can be seen working the hand-operated levers as a lady in summer dress approaches the white footbridge. A small boat is beached on the bank. The first lock-keeper's cottage was built in 1811 half a mile downstream close to Abingdon bridge.

Salter's steamers still provide twice-daily river trips between Abingdon and Oxford, but the lock itself is greatly altered. The modern lock-keeper's house was built in 1928; the wooden bridge has been replaced by a culvert, the banks have been shored up to prevent erosion, and there is a substantial jetty where boats can moor while waiting to pass through the lock. Shorts and shirts are today's preferred summer wear.

A rowing boat in Abingdon Lock in 1937. The flower displays were as important then as they are today, with bold tubs of flowers to brighten up the lock-side (right) and densely planted borders (left). The lock gates were still hand operated at this date.

The lock now has a backdrop of tall trees and shrubs. Occasional rowing boats still pass through, but motor cruisers and narrow-boats are more popular nowadays. The modern lock gates are operated mechanically by hydraulic rams which were installed in the winter of 1966/67.

The frozen weir in the Great Frost of February 1895. The ice was so thick that a horse and cart was driven from Sutton Courtenay to Abingdon over the frozen river. The first lock was built by Sir George Stonhouse in 1649 and rebuilt in 1802. The weir was built in 1833 and rebuilt in 1893, two years before this picture was taken.

Elizabeth Drury, who took many of the photographs for this book, is pictured crossing the weir with her grand-children, Griff and Bryn. There was formerly a ferry boat crossing above the lock, commemorated in the name Ferryboat Field. The gangway was constructed in the 1960s and provides a popular circular walk. The modern weir allows better control of the water flow which helps to minimise flooding.

3
St Helen's Church and the Thames to the Marina

The archway beside St. Helen's Church in 1907. The path leads to the almshouses, the churchyard and St. Helen's Mill. Part of Clarke's clothing factory is visible behind the railings. The clothing factory, the railings and the finial of the pineapple have all now disappeared.

The spire and two aisles of St. Helen's Church, c.1860. The children in this very early photograph are standing by the end of the wall beside the garden of Long Alley almshouses. Two more figures are near the gate into the churchyard.

A young couple enjoy a walk through the churchyard. The wall to the left of the gate has gone and only the church spire is now visible behind the trees.

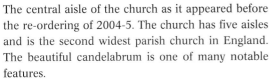

The central aisle of the church as it appeared before the re-ordering of 2004-5. The church has five aisles and is the second widest parish church in England. The beautiful candelabrum is one of many notable features.

The church has recently been re-ordered to allow a movable altar table in a central space, surmounted by an elegant modern corona - part of a comprehensive schedule of alterations.

St. Helen's Mill in 1955. The buildings belonged to the St. Helen's Milling Co. which supplied animal feedstuffs. The river Ock, which provided water power for the mill, is on the left.

The warehouse on the left was converted into private accommodation in 1981, but the company continued trading from the Mill House until the 1990s. The building just visible on the right housed Abingdon's first National School, a Church of England elementary school established in 1823 by public subscription. A potter, Cyril Braunton, had his pottery workshop here from the 1970s to the 1990s. All these buildings have now been converted into housing.

The River Ock beside St. Helen's Mill, c.1967. The bridge led to a stable beside meadows which were used for grazing.

The brick building just visible (above right) has been partly demolished to give access round the side of the mill, and the stable has been converted into a house adjoining the Mill Paddock development (see p.48).

The garden of Long Alley almshouses photographed by Henry Taunt in the 1880s. The Fraternity of the Holy Cross, a medieval charity, built the almshouses in 1446 to accommodate seven poor men and six poor women. They have been continuously occupied ever since.

In the 16th century the Fraternity was reformed as Christ's Hospital, the Abingdon charity which still exists today and runs all the town's almshouses. All the almshouses have now been modernised. Here a ninety two year old resident enjoys the autumn sunshine in the peace of Long Alley gardens where the elderly almsfolk once grew vegetables.

Henry Taunt's classic view of St. Helen's Wharf, c.1880. The clothing factory with its tall chimney and St. Helen's spire rise up behind Long Alley (left) and Brick Alley almshouses. The old Anchor pub (centre) advertises boats for hire and a landing stage for the Queen's Hotel. The buildings beyond the pub were known as the 'Almshouses-over-the-water'.

An engraving of St. Helen's Wharf from the 1878 edition of Alfred Rimmer's 'Pleasant spots around Oxford'. The illustration shows the old Anchor Inn with steps leading down to the landing stage for patrons of the Queen's Hotel. Tall elms and a haystack reflect the agricultural nature of the meadows on the opposite bank of the river.

All the buildings between the road and the river were demolished by Christ's Hospital in 1884 to create this pleasant, tree-shaded promenade. The Anchor pub and the almshouses were rebuilt on the other side of the road, to the left of Long Alley almshouses.

Henry Taunt re-photographed the scene in 1885 with the new pub and almshouse (centre). In the foreground, boats are under construction in the Davis Engineering Works. The firm built canal barges and steam pleasure boats for use on the Thames, as well as ocean-going tugs which were fitted out near the mouth of the Thames.

A flotilla of Canada geese swims past the graceful willow tree growing on the site of the former Engineering Works (above) which is now the Margaret Brown garden. The entrance to the Wilts & Berks canal was in front of the stone wall.

A large boathouse on Wilsham Road in the 1960s. The Wilts & Berks canal, promoted in 1790 and opened in 1810, joined the Thames via a lock under the Nissen hut. The canal basin lay behind the large building, St. Helen's Ironworks, just visible on the right - part of the Engineering Works which later became the Hygienic Laundry (see Chapter 4).

The boathouse has gone and the whole area round the canal basin has been developed for housing, starting with Wharf Close in 1971 and more recently the conversion of the old laundry. The steel shuttering marks the former canal mouth.

Main picture: A water tournament on 'Wilsom' (Wilsham) Reach on 6 July 1893 in celebration of the Duke and Duchess of York's wedding. Marquees and a grandstand have been erected on the meadows and cheering crowds line the river bank.

Left: Today's celebrations are no less popular and colourful. This picture shows the same stretch of river with one of the annual Dragon Boat races organised by the Abingdon Vesper Rotary Club.

A school eight in training on Wilsham Reach in 1993. Rowing has been an important sport at both Abingdon School and Radley College since Victorian times. The motor cruisers are for hire from Red Line Cruisers at 'Ferry Boat House' (centre) formerly the ferryman's hut.

Abingdon School fours set out from the school boathouse on Wilsham Road for a practice session on the Thames in the 1930s. A pair of semi-detached council houses stands out in splendid isolation.

There are houses and bungalows along the length of the road now. The pair of semi-detached houses has been extended, altered and painted white and the boathouse has been replaced by bungalows. In 2003 Abingdon School built a splendid new boathouse further down Wilsham Road. It is said to be the largest timber-framed building in Europe.

Wilsham Road looking towards the town in 1904. The boathouse seen on p.39 stands out prominently, here with an awning. A large house, Kingsland Lodge, stood behind the stone wall on the left.

The trees on the south side of the river now hide the view of the town. The grassy river bank has been piled and concreted to provide moorings. Wilsham Road is now like any other urban street with tarmac, street lights and busy traffic, but the river is still a source of peaceful enjoyment.

The view across one of the flooded gravel pits towards Abingdon in 1985. The spire of St. Helen's Church is just visible above the large building (centre) with the roofs of houses in Andersey Way on the left. Peep-o'-Day Lane, the old summer track to Sutton Courtenay, led past Corporation Farm, the gravel pits and the sewage works.

North Quay, the first part of the Marina development, was built in the mid 1980s. The medley of rooflines and house styles was designed to mimic a traditional townscape. The only point of reference in these two views is the tip of St. Helen's church spire.

4
Caldecott, Drayton Road and Saxton Road

Delighted crowds welcome the procession of MG cars and floats as they enter the MG sports ground in Caldecott Road on 8th September 1979, to celebrate 50 years of MG production in Abingdon. The Golden Jubilee celebrations ran from 1st to 9th September, but were marred by the parent company's announcement that the factory was about to be closed.

An aerial view of Abingdon's riverside setting in the 1950s. The river Ock runs past St Helen's Mill and Long Alley Almshouses to join the Thames near the Hygienic Laundry building on Wilsham Road (bottom right). The large buildings behind the mill near St Helen's Church are Clarke's Clothing Factory, part of which burned down in 1944. Caldecott Road runs through the row of trees in the foreground.

A view across the meadows to St. Helen's Mill (centre) and Long Alley Almshouses (right) in 1980. The building behind the notice board is the stable on p. 35, now converted to a house.

Mill Paddock, a 1983 housing development on the site, has houses built on stilts because of regular flooding. It is seen here during the floods of 2003. Two McCarthy & Stone retirement homes, Mill Stream Court and Cygnet Court, and Manor Court retirement bungalows, occupy the rest of the site.

The old Hygienic Laundry at the time of its closure in 1976. The laundry was established in the premises of the former St. Helen's Ironworks (see Chapter 3), one of the industries which sprang up around the canal basin at the bottom of Caldecott Road after the opening of the Wilts & Berks Canal.

The laundry was succeeded by Reynold's Office Equipment in 1977, followed by Hewden's Tool Hire Centre. The site was sold for a housing development which was completed in 2001.

Caldecott Road with its avenue of young trees, probably around 1880. Caldecott House is behind the wall on the left. On the right is the Wilts & Berks canal with a swing bridge leading to the canal basin and surrounding industrial buildings. The canal was already in decline by this date and carrying very little traffic.

The canal fell out of use in 1906 and was filled in during the First World War. It is now a pleasant green space, popular with dog walkers. The houses of Bailie Close can be seen through the trees (left).

Caldecott House, from a sale catalogue of 1935. It was for many years the home of the Hyde family, the original owners of the clothing factory in West St. Helen Street. The last private owner of Caldecott House, Major General Bailie, died in 1918. The house became a hotel in 1938 but was requisitioned by the Air Ministry in 1940. It was acquired by the Dr. Barnardo's charity in 1945 for a children's home.

The Dr. Barnardo's home was a much-loved local charity supported by popular fund-raising events; former residents and staff still meet for an annual reunion. When the home closed in 1972 the house was demolished and replaced by the St. Amand Drive housing estate. (Almeric de St. Amand was a Norman Lord of St. Helen's Manor.) Major General Bailie is commemorated in Bailie Close, pictured here.

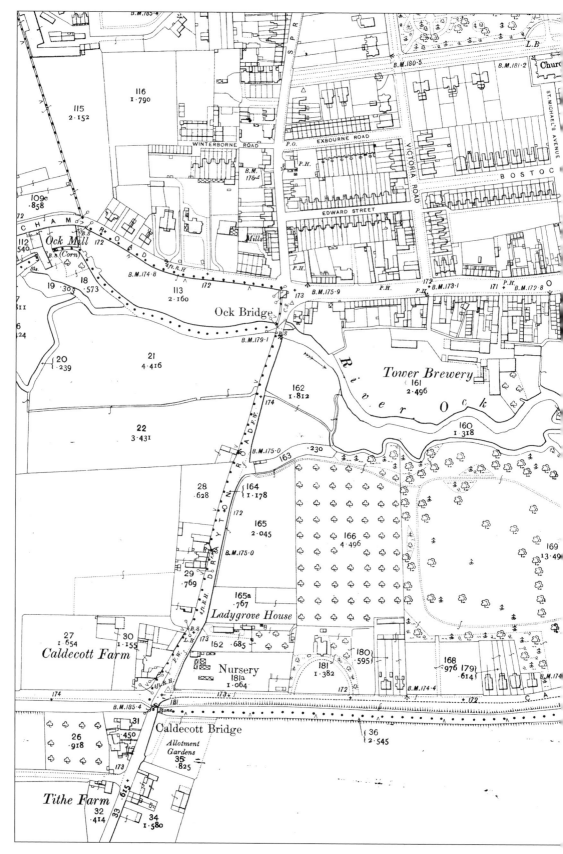

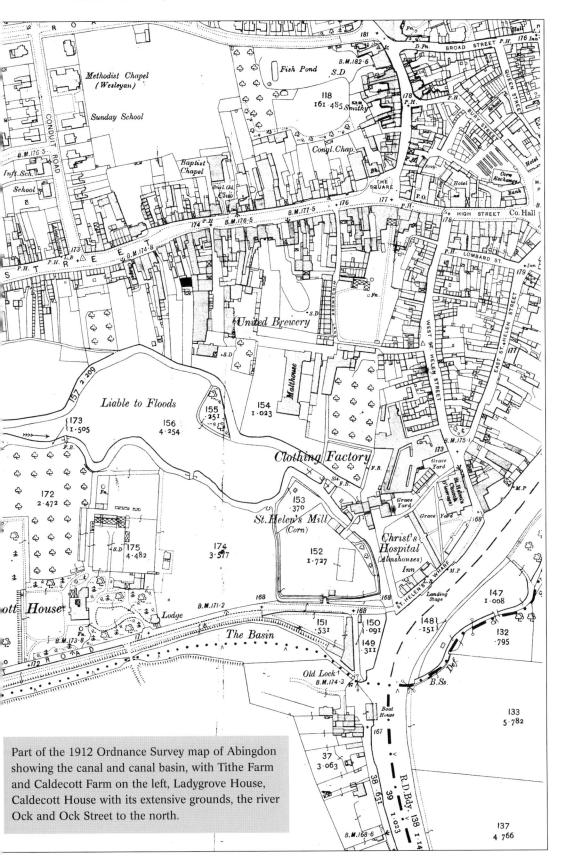

Part of the 1912 Ordnance Survey map of Abingdon showing the canal and canal basin, with Tithe Farm and Caldecott Farm on the left, Ladygrove House, Caldecott House with its extensive grounds, the river Ock and Ock Street to the north.

The junction of Caldecott Road and Drayton Road with the bridge over the former Wilts & Berks canal, which had already fallen out of use when this photograph was taken. The bridge was demolished and replaced by a culvert in 1912. The buildings of Tithe Farm are on the left.

The Tithe Farm buildings have disappeared, but the house behind the bridge (above) can still be seen between the two tall lamp-posts (centre). The service road on the left is on the line of the canal.

The Drayton Road approach to the old canal bridge before its demolition in 1912. Tithe Farm is on the extreme left.

Drayton Road today, looking towards the roundabout at the junction with Caldecott Road. The removal of the bridge allowed the road to be levelled, while new houses, pavements and road furniture have transformed the previous view.

Drayton Road in the 1960s. The garage on the left was then an Esso service station advertising Green Shield stamps. The toll house juts out into the road beyond the Ladygrove Farm buildings, centre right.

The old toll house on Drayton Road.

Drayton Road in 2006. The Cross Roads Renault Garage which formerly occupied the site on the left had relocated to other areas by this date, but the site was still being used to sell commercial vehicles. It is now being developed for housing. The former Hartwell's Rover Garage on the right no longer sells petrol and is now a Hartwell's Citroen and Ford Dealership.

Crowds of children add to the spectacle of this flood on the Drayton Road, probably in June 1903. The white house in the middle distance is Ladygrove House. The door and upper window of the toll house are just visible beyond the barns on the right.

The same view during the spectacular floods of July 2007. Both photographs were taken with the photographer standing on the Ock Bridge.

Recently-built council houses in Saxton Road c.1936. This was the first estate to be built by the Corporation to re-house inhabitants of the old 'courts' in the town centre, when many of these were demolished in a 1930s slum clearance programme.

The houses have modern replacement windows and the estate looks more attractive now with its mature trees and shrubs.

5
Marcham Road, Spring Road and Albert Park

A procession of MG cars moves down Cemetery Road from the new MG factory in 1929. The MG Car Company took over part of the Spring Road works of the Pavlova Leather Company when the car company moved from Oxford to Abingdon.

An aerial photograph of Marcham Road and the MG factory site in the early 1970s. Marcham Road runs from left to right at the bottom of the photograph. Cows are grazing on the meadows beside the river Ock. The Ock Mill (centre foreground) has a large extension built by Objex Ltd., the company which was then occupying it. Opposite is the main entrance to the MG site, with a factory road leading away from it. To the right of this road are the large MG buildings and (far right) the Pavlova Leather Works. To the left are more MG buildings, a large car park filled with MG cars off the production line sandwiched between extensive allotments, and (centre left) the buildings of the Marcham Road Hospital. Colwell Drive now runs on the line of the factory road. The whole area to the left of the road is now occupied by Fairacres retail park and Nuffield Way industrial estate, with the new police station on the opposite side, at the junction with Marcham Road. The A34 By-Pass now runs through the fields to the west and north of the MG site. Part of Shippon village and the runways of RAF Abingdon can be seen beyond.

The main offices and some of the factory buildings of the MG Car Company on Marcham Road on its final day in 1980.

After the company closed, strenuous efforts were made to keep at least some of the buildings – possibly as an MG museum – but without success. The new Thames Valley Police Station now occupies this part of the site.

The old County Police Station in Bridge Street, in the town centre, photographed in 1995. It was replaced by the new police station.

A constable stands in front of the imposing new Thames Valley Police Station which was opened by the Home Secretary, Jack Straw, in 2000.

A bird's-eye view of Marcham Road looking towards its junction with Ock Street in 1977. The main entrance to the MG car factory is in the centre foreground. Ock Mill and Ock Mill House, opposite, are now a Beefeater Steakhouse restaurant. There is a Premier Travel Inn on the site of the small barn beside the Mill House, and a new Care Home for the elderly, Abingdon Court, opened alongside in 2007.

A view of Ock Mill House with the adjoining mill building and small barn in 1987. A new roundabout, defining the entrance to the recently-opened Abingdon Business Park (left), has been built in front of the former main entrance to the MG site.

A Travel Inn (right) has replaced the old barn beside Ock Mill House, with a new road, Colwell Drive, making this a busy junction. McDonald's Restaurant is behind the photographer.

Marcham Road looking east in 1987. The few houses in Marcham Road, including the Victorian cottages (left), enjoyed uninterrupted views across the meadows to the River Ock.

The rural scene has given way to an urban landscape. The Ock Mill Close housing development (right) was built in 1996. A new road sign shows the double roundabout at Ock Bridge, now one of the busiest junctions in Abingdon.

Marcham Road under water in the Great Flood of 15th November 1894. The Ock Mill and Ock Mill House are in the background. The pollarded willows to the left mark the course of the River Ock. Thomas Dean 'Timber & Slate Merchant &c.' had a sawmill and yard at 2-4 Marcham Road off the photograph to the right. He also sold wash-basins and pipes, which are piled against the end of no.6 Marcham Road, possibly also part of his premises.

The double roundabout at the junction of the Drayton and Marcham roads. The houses of Ock Mill Close fill the meadows on the left. No.6 Marcham Road has for many years been the headquarters of the Abingdon Drama Club, but the balconies, flowers and railings have all disappeared.

The view up Spring Road from the Ock Street junction during the Great Flood of 1894. Thomas Dean's sawmill is on the left. Flooding occurred regularly along Ock Street, but exceptional floods such as those of 1891, 1894 and 1947 attracted special attention. The children may have come out of school just in time to pose for the photographer.

Residents wade through floodwater during the floods of July 2007. Much of the town was impassable as Marcham Road, Drayton Road, Spring Road and Ock Street were all closed to traffic. The view is little changed except that most of the houses now have television aerials. The buildings of the West End Sawmills, still in commercial use, are now occupied by Abingdon Kitchens & Bathrooms and Osborn's model shop. The White Horse inn sign has been moved to make room for an extension to the public house.

A postcard view of Spring Road, c.1910. The Victorian terraced houses give the street a unified appearance. The horse and cart and hand carts were still the main forms of transport for people and goods at this date, but a van can also be seen.

Today, cars and vans have replaced horses and carts, there are neat brick walls instead of railings, and house owners' individuality is expressed with painted walls, new front doors and modern windows.

Knight's Chapel Works at 13 Spring Road in 1976. Garden ornaments and heavy goods were sold from these premises. Knight's main shop was at 11 Spring Road on the opposite corner of Edward Street, selling electrical appliances and paints, etc. The previous occupant of no.13 was Luker & Sons, decorators and plumbers. In the 19th century the building had been used as a chapel for the Primitive Methodists, hence the name; they moved here from their old premises at 47 The Vineyard.

The chapel building has been transformed with the removal of the front porch and old windows. Brightly painted, neatly landscaped and with a new front entrance, it now houses Abingdon Beds.

Spring Road looking south towards Ock Street in 1976. The Prince of Wales pub is prominent in the foreground. The pub opened in 1869 and seems to have been purpose-built to serve new housing in the area. The shop just visible on the corner of Edward Street near the bottom of the road, formerly Cullen's grocers, is Knight's electrical shop.

The Prince of Wales closed in 1988; it became the headquarters of the Abingdon Royal British Legion club in 1991. The chimneys have been lowered and an extension has been built in the garden beyond, but little else has changed.

Exbourne Road looking east in 1948 with the spire of Trinity Church in the distance. The north side of Exbourne Road was built in 1906 by Christ's Hospital as part of the Albert Park estate. In the 1950s the corner shop was the West End branch of Rant & Tombs, grocers, who also had branches in Ock Street and the Oxford Road. From the 1960s it was known as the West End Stores.

The street in 2004 is full of parked cars and the architectural unity of the terraces has been broken by modern replacement windows and doors. Fortunately the electricity poles are less intrusive than formerly.

The West End Stores and Post Office closed in 2005, a sad loss of a valuable local amenity. The shop has been converted into living accommodation.

The Spring Road cemetery in 1873. It was laid out in 1860/61 with both an Anglican and a Non-Conformist chapel. The former Superintendent's lodge is just visible on the left. The cemetery occupies the land between Cemetery Road and Spring Gardens.

The old cemetery today. More space was needed as the population of Abingdon expanded, and a new burial ground to the north of Spring Gardens is now in use.

Tollgate Cottage at the junction of Faringdon Road and Spring Road (right) in 1939. This triangular plot, formerly known as Trinity Close, was the probable site of Trinity Chapel in Abbey times and burials have been found there. Several toll houses were built on the main approaches to Abingdon when turnpike roads were constructed in the 18th century.

The toll house was pulled down in 1948. Several houses now stand behind a thick hedge at the road junction.

The main entrance to RAF Abingdon in 1992. Handsome emblems crown the two gateposts and the site is protected by simple barriers. The station opened in 1932, originally as an operational bomber station. It was later notable as the home of No.1 Parachute Training School providing personnel for the 'Falcons', the famous RAF Display Team, and for the annual air shows.

In the 1980s the Ministry of Defence decided to close the airfield and sell it off, but there was a change of plan. It was taken over by the army in 1992 and is now the home of two regiments of the Royal Logistic Corps. Known as Dalton Barracks after James Langley Dalton, one of the VC heroes of Rorke's Drift in the Boer War, the entrance is now barred by heavy steel gates and guarded by armed soldiers.

A solitary gentleman contemplates the view near the impressive statue of Prince Albert, after whom the Albert Park was named. The monument, designed by Gibbs of Oxford, was erected on the highest point of the park and inaugurated on July 1st 1865. The house on the right is 'Whitefield' one of the first houses to be built on Park Crescent after the park was laid out in the 1860s. It is now part of Abingdon School.

Young families enjoy a sunny afternoon beneath the watchful eye of Prince Albert. The occasion pictured here was a sponsored walk organised by a local primary school.

Albert Park in its Victorian heyday, with neatly clipped shrubs and colourful bedding plants. The cannon, a relic from the Crimean War, once stood outside the Abbey gateway. It was removed for scrap metal, together with the park railings, during World War II but was never used. It was then stored in the Abbey grounds and is said to be buried somewhere in the Abbey meadows.

The park has a more natural feel today, and the formal beds have been sacrificed to provide a car park for the Abingdon Bowling Club.

Bostock Road had a rather bleak appearance in the 1930s, with its pollarded trees and absence of shrubs in the front gardens. Although part of the same late Victorian development as Exbourne Road it is noticeably different, with its wide, tree-lined grass verges and villa-style houses on the left. The terrace on the right, known as Tesdale Terrace, was built in 1895 as model cottages for artisans.

Today the road has a pleasant, suburban air with its well-tended grass verges and leafy trees. Bostock Road was formerly known as Bostock Avenue; the name was changed around 1934.

Girls in pinafores are pictured in the yard of the new County Council School in Bostock Road. The teacher on the right is holding a skipping rope. Originally known as the British School, it was founded by the Baptist Church in 1824 in a building to the right of the church entrance in Ock Street. The school was taken over by the School Board for Abingdon in 1899 and moved to new premises in Bostock Road, seen here, in 1902.

Now called Carswell Community Primary School, it has expanded to accommodate a growing number of pupils, many from army families at Dalton Barracks (formerly RAF Abingdon). Today's young children are less formally dressed and are taught in mixed classes of boys and girls.

6
Ock Street,
the South Side

A view of Ock Street looking towards the Square in 1906. The shop-fronts with their old gas-lights are festooned with goods. A lad stands on the corner of Winsmore Lane, (right foreground) and beyond, the buildings form an unbroken line into the Square. The gabled building, just visible at the end on the right, is the Square House which stood on the site of the famous Lamb Inn. It was demolished when the Regal Cinema was built in 1935. The smoke from a steam engine can be seen in the High Street behind the hand-carts and pony and trap.

Holmes (formerly Trotman), the popular bakery and café in 1985. The Holmes family came to Abingdon in 1927. Their first bakery was at 100 Ock Street – one of six in Ock Street at that date. The buildings to the left of Holmes are the offices of the Courier newspaper.

Holmes closed in the 1990s and is now the Dil Raj Indian restaurant. The Courier offices are now occupied by Forrester's Hair Care.

Ock Street looking west after the Great Blizzard of 25th April 1908. Two feet of snow with drifts six feet deep were left after 24 hours of heavy snow and high winds. On the left is the imposing 18th century Clock House with its stable yard. Beyond are Coxeter's ironmongers shop and Vernon Whitehead's garage. Coxeter's furnishing department on the north side of the street was opened in the 1880s. By 1908 it had become Coxeters & Andrew.

The junction of Ock Street and Stratton Way in 2006 during road-works for the Abingdon Integrated Transport Scheme (Abits). The Clock House was converted to offices in the 1980s. The old gas lamps have disappeared, and further down the south side of the street, the tall gabled building of Vernon Whitehead's garage has been rebuilt. The north side looks very different after the rebuilding of Coxeter's premises (right).

The Georgian Tea House in 1942 occupying part of the Clock House. Coxeter's original ironmongers shop next door has become Brind, Gillingham & Co. with the rebuilt garage beyond.

This page from a 1948 student guide book advertises the Georgian House Café at 28 Ock Street. The Clock House building was much admired by Nikolaus Pevsner, especially its elegant curved staircase.

MORNING COFFEE
AND
AFTERNOON TEAS

The Georgian House
28 OCK STREET, ABINGDON
(PHONE ABINGDON 594)

OPEN ALL THE WEEK EXCEPT WEDNESDAYS
AND OPEN ALL DAY SUNDAYS

SMALL PARTIES CATERED FOR

THE Georgian House is unique with its beautiful panelling and staircase, attributed to William Kent, and should be seen by all who visit Abingdon.

In 1951 the ironmongers shop was bought by Mr Bertram Beadle and his wife. It is seen here in the 1960s. The garage next door has become H.V. Eyles & Son.

Beadles, a much-loved business, closed in 2000 shortly after the closure of Morland's Brewery. The site was developed for housing but the façade has been retained. Note the dormer windows visible on p.84 which have been re-instated. The garage next door is now Merityre (formerly Wellaway's). This site has been serving the needs of motorists for over a hundred years.

This 1947 photograph shows an unbroken line of buildings, 44-48 Ock Street. The tall gabled buildings on the far left were formerly Morland's offices and the home of the Head Brewer. The latter is now the Brewery Tap pub.

Numbers 44-48 Ock Street were demolished in 1962 to create a new wide entrance into Morland's site. The gable end of the Brewery Tap stands out beyond the entrance. This 17th century building was given a mock-Elizabethan façade c.1905. In 1993 it was converted into a public house to compensate for the loss of the Warrick Arms and the Crown opposite. The building on the right is a new town house, part of Cooper's Yard.

Morland's Brewery yard in 1995 with a large articulated lorry in front of the new distribution building. It was a great shock to the town when this old-established Abingdon business was sold to Greene King, and the brewing of Morland's beers was transferred to Bury St Edmunds in Suffolk. When the brewery closed in 1999 some of the plant was shipped to Russia.

Several of the old brewery buildings were converted into flats and apartments and the rest of the site has been developed for new housing by Berkeley Homes. The new road is called Cooper's Yard.

The brewhouse in 1992 with empty kegs stored in the yard.

A condition of the planning consent for this development was that some of the important brewery buildings should be retained. Here, the brewhouse (centre right) and new housing sit comfortably together. The new brewhouse (extreme right) was only built in 1995.

A drawing of old cottages at 54-62 Ock Street in 1816. In 1900 William Barnett Junior bought no. 54 Ock Street and moved his Mineral Water Factory there from Bath Street. Called the 'Brooklyn Works', it also had a wholesale confectionery department making sweets and toffees.

Nos. 54 and 56 Ock Street in the 1930s. Thomas Leach started his printing business in 1901 and moved it to 54 Ock Street in 1937. No. 56 with its striking Art Deco façade was occupied by Rant & Tombs, grocers, for many years.

Leach's the Printers occupied 54 Ock Street until 2008. The house is barely recognisable from the one in the drawing. The railings and balcony have been removed and a carriage entrance driven through the left-hand side of the building. Nos. 56-62 were demolished in 1969 to accommodate the Post Office Engineering Department, now occupied by M J A Consulting.

A view of Ock Street looking east in 1890, taken
near the junction with Conduit Road by the Oxford
photographer Henry Taunt.
On the left, J. Leonard offers a wide range of services
including plumbing and glazing. On the right is the
old Methodist Chapel and two doors beyond, a dairy
shop selling butter and cheese.

Above. Most of the buildings on the right of the main picture, including the Methodist Chapel, were demolished to make way for the entrance to the Royal Mail sorting office and Ballard's, now F. Knight's premises.

Below. The Methodist Chapel, built in 1845, served originally as a Wesleyan chapel until Trinity Methodist Church was built in Conduit Road in 1875. The Ock Street chapel was then occupied by the Primitive Methodists from Spring Road (p. 71). The building was in use as a Methodist Youth Club in 1951.

Harry Giles and two of his three sons outside the family's general store at 80 Ock Street, c.1910. The property included a large barn at least 100 feet long, five cottages and about 1 acre of land. All three Giles boys enlisted in the First World War, including the youngest, who lied about his age so that he could join his brothers. All three were killed – a devastating tragedy for the family. Their names can be seen on the War Memorial, together with other relatives.

Eighteen-year-old Emily Giles in the doorway of the family's general store at 80 Ock Street in 1917.

Cottages, barn and orchard have long since disappeared and no. 80 is now a private house, although it still has the large ground-floor shop window seen above. On the left is F. Knight & Sons builders' merchant (formerly Ballard's agricultural machinery). A tool hire centre and other businesses occupy the yard behind.

This map of Ock Street shows the extensive Giles smallholding opposite Conduit Road, with its large barn, and five cottages along the street frontage not far from the Wesleyan Chapel. The family kept at least 50 pigs, 3 or 4 cows, chickens and ducks in the orchard, with grazing for several horses. The barn was believed to have been used as a theatre, and is referred to as the 'old theatre' barn by local historian Agnes Baker ('Historic Abingdon' p.122). Note the row of tiny Baker's Cottages (left) contrasting with 'The Acacias' (later called Helenstowe) in its large garden, now the Conservative Club. The cottages were probably Court 10 which ran behind Miles the baker at no.100 Ock Street, later Holmes bakery.

The Abingdon Traditional Morris Dancers performing in June 1956 on the occasion of their annual celebration to elect the 'mayor' of Ock Street. Left to right, John 'Slim' Mooring (fool), Ernie Constance, Brian Clarke, Tom Hemmings, Charlie Brett, Frank Jordan, Ray Hemmings.

All the old buildings in this section of Ock Street, from no. 100, Holmes Bakery, to 146 next to the Cross Keys public house, have been knocked down. Most of the space is now occupied by the Fire Station, with Mayott House home for the elderly beyond.

The Cross Keys pub and Walters Cafe, 148-154 Ock Street, in 1976. The Cross Keys is the 'home' of the Traditional Morris Men. It has the only pub sign in Abingdon with a religious connotation – the keys to the Kingdom of Heaven, held by St. Peter.

These buildings have changed little over the past 30 years apart from some new windows and the removal of a chimney from no. 154. The Cross Keys has a new sign, and Walters Cafe is now the Golden Kitchen, a Chinese take-away. Tonks Brothers, Funeral Directors, have recently moved into premises alongside the Golden Kitchen. The entrance-way just visible immediately to the left of the Golden Kitchen doorway is one of the last surviving examples of a passage-way which led to a 'court' of crowded dwellings behind the street.

Part of the former Tower Brewery buildings (far left) and old cottages at 178-182 Ock Street with Ruddock's fish and chip shop in 1958. Bill Ruddock, his wife Aida and their family came to Abingdon from London in 1919 to take over the fish and chip business. In the early 1900s, this was a fishmongers run by Walter 'Coddy' Steptoe who used to cook fish and chips at weekends in his front room.

Nearly all the buildings from 178 to 238 Ock Street, including the 'Ock Street Horns' public house and 'Pig Row' tenements (p. 99) were demolished in 1961. The first flats at the west end of the new development were occupied in 1963. Ruddock's continued trading while the new flats were being built around it. Their new fish and chip shop (now the China Diner, seen here) which opened in 1966, was an integral part of the new building. The white building beyond, part of the old Tower Brewery, became the British Legion Social Club.

The Ock Street flats which replaced Pig Row (see p. 99) looking west in the 1980s. The large building at the far end is Ock House. By the date of this photograph the flats were already showing their age and looking very drab.

In 1996 the Council embarked on a programme of refurbishment resulting in the transformation seen here. This dramatic picture captures the floods in July 2007 when much of the street was under water, following 24 hours of torrential rain.

A view of the
Michaelmas Fair in the
1950s looking east,
taken from the Big
Wheel which was
always located near the
roundabout by Ock
Bridge. The tall
buildings of Morland's
Brewery stand out
against the skyline, far
right.

The Fair is as popular as
ever, and it is the only
occasion when people
can enjoy Ock Street
free of traffic. It was
originally a hiring fair
for farm labourers and
servants, and is said to
be the longest street fair
in Europe.

7
Ock Street, the North Side

A father and son of the Wiggins family stand in the middle of an empty, traffic-free street by the homes they occupied at nos. 175 and 177 Ock Street (left foreground) c.1910. The row of houses on the right was known as Pig Row because many of the occupants kept a pig in their long back gardens.

Six of Harry and Julia Wiggins's nine children pose around a lamp post at the west end of an almost deserted Ock Street, c.1918. The small barn on the left which belonged to the White Horse public house was once a malthouse. Oriel House, the home and surgery of Dr Baker in the 1920s, is just visible beyond the nineteenth century tenements whose date 1863 is built into the brickwork.

The barn has been altered and the tenements were demolished in the 1980s to enlarge the car park of the White Horse. Oriel House has been replaced by a block of flats, Juniper Court.

Another view of the west end of Ock Street in 1984. The site of Oriel House, part of which was a former Baptist burial ground, was bought by the Quakers who built a meeting house here in 1697. Oriel House was built in 1865; it became the Oriel Hotel in 1953 and was popular with commercial travellers.

The old houses were knocked down not long after the picture above was taken. In 1988 the Oriel Hotel was replaced by Juniper Court, a large block of retirement flats.

Reeves & Son's fish and chip shop, Blake Bros. Corn Merchants and the Air Balloon public house in 1976. The pub was first mentioned in 1788, four years after James Sadler of Oxford's balloon ascents and six years after the original Montgolfier balloon experiments. In the 1890s Blake's premises were also a pub, the Hollybush, and there was a 'New Air Balloon' almost opposite. Beyond are the substantial Victorian houses at the entrance to Victoria Road.

Reeves is now the Salamis Fish Bar, the Corn Merchants is a private house, and the Air Balloon has also been converted into housing. Further houses and flats have been built on the pub's former yard on the corner of Ock Street and Victoria Road.

A terrace of cottages, 145-159 Ock Street, next to Michael Harris, Monumental Masons, in the 1960s. The houses are boarded up ready for demolition. Stimpsons fruiterers shop at no.149 in this row was rebuilt at no.141 (see p.104).

Modern flats have replaced the old cottages. Originally built by the Abingdon charity Christ's Hospital and the Mullard Housing Trust for the elderly and retired, they are now owned by Oxford Citizens Housing Association. Harris's Monumental Masonry business is still operating from the same site. The group of buildings beyond has survived.

143 Ock Street, formerly the Happy Dick public house, in 1958 with a row of old houses beyond. The pub had closed in 1950.

Nos. 109-143 Ock Street in 1976. The houses next to the Happy Dick have been replaced by a new shop, Stimpson's fruiterers and grocery store at 135-141, previously at no. 149. No. 143 is occupied by W J Hall & Son, builders and decorators. The two shops with awnings are Cordell the butcher at no. 131 and Spooner's newsagent next door at no. 129.

Little has changed except that the bollards in the centre of the road have been replaced by a pedestrian crossing. Domino's Pizza now occupies Stimpson's shop.

An attractive row of shops and cottages at 111-129 Ock Street in 1958. Hemmings Brothers cycle shop advertises the 'New Hudson' super steel bicycle. Spooner's newsagent is just visible on the left.

Harold Hemmings in overalls with Alf Hemmings holding a bicycle outside the family cycle shop in the 1920s.

Several different businesses have occupied these premises in recent years including Paterson Recruitment (still at no.121), the Movies video shop, 'Tradition' Afro-Caribbean & Continental shop and the Fantasia Bridal Centre, which has moved from 125, part of Hemming's old shop (now empty), to Cordell's butcher's shop at 131. The newsagent has also closed.

A row of cottages with George Exon's bakery and shop c.1927. Gowring's Garages acquired the end house, no. 111 Ock Street, in 1927 to open a new Ford depot selling Ford cars and Fordson tractors. An advertisement in the North Berks Herald of 23rd September 1927 alerted customers to the imminent arrival of a new model Ford with 'more speed and flexibility and more graceful lines than any low-priced car yet known'. The other buildings seen in the photograph were demolished later as Gowring's expanded.

Gowring's is now Bellinger's Vauxhall garage and showroom.

The Abingdon Morris dancers outside Gowring's garage in the 1950s. Left to right, Ray Hemmings, Leslie Argyle, Frank Jordan, Charlie Brett, Jack Hyde, Johnny Grimsdale. The gabled building next to the garage on the right was Miss Wheeler's house and drapery shop.

Gowring's premises have been rebuilt, and in 1997 Gowring's became Bellinger's Vauxhall dealership. The white gabled houses beyond the drapery shop on the far side of Mayott Road have also been demolished and replaced.

Mr. Warrick's Arms Hotel in 1976. This establishment, which had been trading since 1854, made a lively addition to this part of Ock Street with its hipped roof, striped awnings and distinctive inn sign. It had function rooms for private parties and community events and was popular with a large clientele of 'regulars'. The small shops beyond included Audrey's flower shop, Status Trophies and Mega Bonus white goods.

There were strong objections when the owners, Morlands, closed both Mr Warrick's Arms and the Crown pub nearby. The two pubs were converted as part of a housing development called Crown Mews which was built in 1995. Mr Warrick's Arms is barely recognisable now without its inn sign and colourful awnings. Audrey's flower shop closed in 2003.

An elaborate funeral procession outside W. Enock's premises. White horses were traditionally used for the funeral of a child. Enock's business interests included coal merchants, undertakers and the hire of horse-drawn carriages.

Part of Enock's old premises, no. 75 (now with tile-hung front), survives as a private house as does Pollard's the plumbers at no. 77. No. 81 beyond is still a Funeral Directors. Tomkins' Almshouses are visible beyond the entrance to Conduit Road.

A charming painting of old cottages in Enock's Yard. The spire of Trinity Methodist & United Reform church can be seen in the background.

The cottage (left above) by the entrance to Enock's coal yard, seen here in 1993. The Enocks also sold Christmas trees in season. Some old cottages which formerly stood along the street to the right of the yard entrance were condemned as unfit and demolished in the 1960s.

The coal yard closed in 1998/9 and was redeveloped as Ock Mews, seen here. The church spire is still visible behind the houses.

No. 59 Ock Street, 'Helenstowe' (formerly 'The Acacias') c.1910. This substantial house with its large garden was the home and surgery of Dr. Woodford from 1900-1939. In 1951 the surgery was being run by Dr Fitzgerald O'Connor and Dr Joan Harcourt.

An unidentified officer photographed in the extensive ornamental gardens of Helenstowe in 1915. According to an auction catalogue of 1891, the gardens had an 'Arbour, two Lawns and large fountain and were well planted with fruit trees in full bearing'.

The house became the headquarters of the Abingdon Division Conservative Club in 1973. It was officially opened by Airey Neave, MP for Abingdon, in 1974. The large garden is now the club car park.

The funeral of Harry Wiggins, carpenter and builder, on 28th June 1947. The hearse stands outside 35 Ock Street, the creeper-covered manse of the Baptist Church, with the Cock & Tree public house beyond. Other cars in the cortege wait outside his home and place of business, 39 Ock Street. Gibson's garage with a Shell petrol pump is in the foreground opposite.

Merityre (left), the Abingdon Tyre Specialists, is in Gibson's old premises. The street scene on the north side has hardly changed. The Baptist manse, 35 Ock Street, was completely refurbished in 1995/96. It has become a valuable asset for the Baptist Church and for the wider community, and is used by many local organisations as well as providing a popular venue for coffee and light lunches.

Coxeters furniture shop at 23-25 on the north side of Ock Street in the 1930s. Coxeters first ironmongers shop opened in 1836 on the south side of the street (see p. 84). The furniture shop opened in the 1880s, followed by a cycle depot next to the original shop in 1895.

The buildings on either side of the archway (see above) were demolished in 1969 to make way for the inner relief road, Stratton Way. Coxeters' large, modern department store, now called Coxeter House, was built in 1966/7. It now contains over 20 different businesses, with Stratton's Nightclub on the first floor. Richard Coxeter Furnishing is on the left, with Richard Matthews' plant stall in the space between.

Old barns behind Coxeters' Ock Street frontage. The buildings were accessed through the archway (see previous page) and were probably used to house Coxeters' horses and delivery vans.

The barn on the right, above, was demolished when the inner relief road, Stratton Way, was constructed in 1969. The long barn on the left contains the Warehouse work clothing shop and Scorpion Signs, with the Oracle Snooker Club upstairs. The tall building (centre) houses Seeney's Pet Supplies. The red brick of the Youth and Community Centre, now known as 'The Net', is just visible to the right of a new building (2007). In 2006 Stratton Way was converted to two-way traffic with new bus standing bays.

The east end of Ock Street looking towards the Square in the early 1960s. At this time before Stratton Way was opened there was still two-way traffic in this section of Ock Street, and northbound A34 through traffic was routed along Bath Street where the bus is going. Allee's was one of the last three independent butchers in Abingdon. The shop on the extreme left is 'Elvira B', a popular ladies' dress shop.

Allee's premises were re-built as seen here in 1965. The business closed in 1992 and was replaced by the Spruce Dry Cleaning shop. 'Elvira B' became a French restaurant, the Bistro Celte, which changed to the Limoncello Italian restaurant in 2007.

A rare view of a horse market in the Square in the 1890s. Traditionally used for a sheep or possibly a cattle market, the plane trees were planted in the Square in 1888 after a purpose-built market was created behind Bury Street.

Today the Square has a bright, prosperous appearance with colourful flower beds round the War Memorial and well maintained old buildings. The house on the left of Smart's Fish & Chip shop now shows a timber framed façade.

8
Vineyard and Radley Road

The Red Lion pub in the Vineyard in 2000 with a Morland's delivery van outside. The Red Lion, which closed in 2003, was one of many Abingdon pubs which have been sold for housing in recent years.

The Vineyard looking towards the town centre, c.1950, before the street was redeveloped. The Red Lion pub (left foreground) is overshadowed by the large buildings of the former Lloyd's Academy for boys. A gas lamp stands by the entrance to New Street with a milk float from Candy's Dairy parked nearby.

The Vineyard in the 1960s. The road has been widened following the demolition of the old Lloyds academy building giving a clear view down the street. A BP petrol station (which also repaired cars) has replaced the demolished houses on the left. Another BP petrol station has been built on the right and beyond is a new block of flats, Banbury Court, built in 1962. Old cottages (right and bottom left) are awaiting demolition or refurbishment,

The same view of the Vineyard as those opposite. Almost all the buildings on the left hand side are new. The Red Lion pub and the garage beyond have been replaced by housing. Some of the older buildings on the right hand side survive and Banbury Court at the far end of the street has been refurbished and given a pitched roof.

A newspaper stall run by Hilda and Arthur Pearce outside Abingdon Motors (the BP garage seen on the left in the picture opposite) in the early 1960s. From 1965-1972 this was Hartwells garage; in 1973 it became St Helen's Garage and later Motorvine. The Pearces ran their paper stall throughout this period.

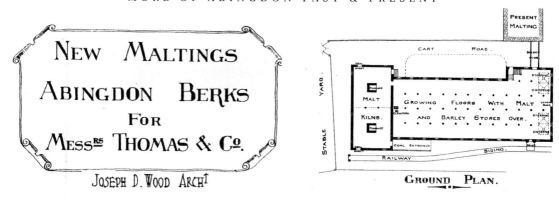

Architects' drawings of the New Maltings in the Vineyard featured in The Building News of January 27th 1905. Railway sidings link the different buildings to the Abingdon Branch railway line seen in the foreground, with the end of the station platform at the far left.

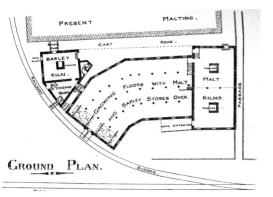

Waitrose car park occupies the area of the main railway track while new apartments and town houses now fill the malthouse site and the former gas works nearby.

New Street, the Vineyard, c.1950 with Basil Pearce, son of Arthur and Hilda Pearce, riding his bicycle down the road. The houses behind the fence on the left were knocked down when the Abingdon Motors garage was built in the 1960s.

Arthur Pearce stands beside his son's Morris car in New Street in the early 1960s. The wall of the Red Lion pub is on the right.

Beryl Horne (nee Pearce) outside the family home in New Street. Mrs Horne was known to generations of local children as a school crossing lady, first at Dunmore School and later at John Mason School. These cottages were built by the nearby Maltings to house their workers in the early years of the 20th century. The modern houses beyond were built on the former garage site and those on the right occupy the site of the Red Lion public house (see p. 117).

The top of the Vineyard near its junction with Radley Road, c.1969. A few shops survived at this end of the street, including the Abingdon DIY Shop (formerly the Windsor Fish Saloon), Elderfields Wavy Line grocery and a small sweet shop, formerly Mrs Belcher's wool shop.

Unlike most of the rest of the street, these buildings have scarcely changed in appearance. The DIY shop is now the Pedal Power cycle shop and Elderfields is Mr Lee's Hair Design Studio. The white cottage on the left was the Old Row Barge pub which closed in 1963.

The Catholic Church of Our Lady and St. Edmund on the corner of the Oxford and Radley Roads, c.1878. The original schoolhouse is just visible on the left. The church, manse and school were built by Sir George Stonhouse of Radley Park in 1857 after his conversion to Catholicism. The railed-in triangle of shrubs in the foreground stood at the road junction. The building on the right was part of Vineyard Farm.

The church's ornate steeple has been replaced by a simple bell tower, and a roundabout regulates the traffic at this busy junction. The former schoolhouse is now used as a church hall.

The tall brick house on the right opposite the church on the corner of the Vineyard and Radley Road is 'The Paddocks', formerly part of Vineyard Farm. The stone barn beside the house was one of the farm buildings. From 1884 the farm was occupied by the Jackman family who in 1910 started breeding and training polo ponies. The stud farm finally closed in the late 1950s, but two of the Jackman sisters, Betsy and Emmy, were still living in 'The Paddocks'. The three-acre former farm site, lying between the gas works and the Henry Booth leather factory, was acquired in 1960 by the Longworth Scientific Instrument Co. (later Penlon Ltd.) which moved there from the old carpet factory by Abingdon Bridge.

When Penlon relocated to the Science Park off Audlett Drive in 2003 the Radley Road site was sold for the Kingsoak Homes housing development, Penlon Place. The stone barn was demolished to make way for their temporary sales office which was removed in May 2007.

Victorian terraced houses on the Radley Road, photographed c.1910. There is a pavement and gas street lighting, but the roadway has not yet been made up.
This row of houses was formerly known as Barton Terrace and those beyond as Convent Close.

A close-up view of no.81, the third house from the right in the previous picture, with a tricycle and elderly gentleman outside. No.81 was at one time a dame school.

The street today. The railings were probably removed as part of the 1939-1945 war effort and have mostly not been replaced. The terrace appears little changed apart from the chimneys.

The Warren, a substantial gentleman's residence on the Radley Road, c.1982. The last private owners were Sir George and Lady Dashwood. In 1930 the house became a hospital, replacing the old cottage hospital in Bath Street. The Warren Hospital had men's, women's and children's wards, an operating theatre, x-ray and therapy departments and a three-bed maternity ward. In 1952 the general hospital services were transferred to Marcham Road and the Warren became a maternity hospital serving Abingdon and the surrounding area.

The Warren is fondly remembered by many local mothers who had their babies there. The maternity unit was transferred to Marcham Road in 1968, and the Warren became a geriatric hospital. This closed in 1978 and the house was eventually demolished in 1982 to build the Warren housing estate, seen here.

The area around Abingdon is rich in prehistoric sites, one of the most notable being Barrow Hills, a series of former burial mounds between Abingdon and Radley, off the Radley Road. These were excavated by the Oxford Archaeological Unit and Reading University prior to building the Eason Drive housing development. The dig also uncovered a Roman cemetery of the 2nd to 4th centuries AD (possibly relating to Barton Court Farm Roman villa nearby) and early Saxon houses or sunken huts. This Open Day on the site in September 1983, organised by the Abingdon Area Archaeological & Historical Society and the Oxford Archaeological Unit, attracted a large number of visitors. The fence marks the line of the newly built Audlett Drive. The house and barns of Wick Hall are visible in the left background.

The houses of the Eason Drive estate now occupy the site.

Mrs Josephine Dockar-Drysdale in a governess cart outside the front door of Wick Hall, c.1902. The maids are holding two of her baby daughters, Catherine and Enid. For much of its history the estate (first mentioned as 'la Wyk' in 1284) was virtually self-sufficient with its own dairy and brew-house. It was leased to a John Badcock in 1797; his family lived and farmed there until 1882 when the formidable Josephine Dockar-Drysdale moved from London to Wick Hall. The Badcocks remained tenants on the estate for another hundred years, until the retirement in 1982 of John's great-great-great-grandson, George Badcock.

The present owner, Patrick Dockar-Drysdale, outside the same front door in 2006. The door is now painted white and the lower window to the right of the door has been reinstated. This charming Queen Anne style house was built around 1739 for Mrs Elizabeth Tomkins, a member of the wealthy Baptist family of Abingdon maltsters, and was extended by Josephine Dockar-Drysdale in the 1880s. The gardens of Wick Hall are opened annually to the public.

Barton Court, seen here around 1881. The Manor of Barton was the original land-holding of Abingdon Abbey and is named in the Domesday Book of 1086. The ruin on the left is that of an earlier manor house which had been rebuilt after the dissolution. The Reade family who owned Barton Court were royalists during the civil war. King Charles I and Queen Henrietta Maria said their last farewells here in 1864 before the Queen escaped to France. The house was subsequently burned down in an attack on Abingdon, leaving the ruin seen here.

The house and land were bought by Our Lady's Convent in 1926 to provide a school sports field. In 1930 the house became an old people's home run by the nuns. It eventually became uneconomic and was demolished in 1967. The area was developed for housing in the early 1980s. The ruin now stands in open ground near a children's playing area, surrounded by the houses of Sherwood Avenue.

The junction of Audlett Drive and Barton Lane in 1986, shortly before the development of the Abingdon Science Park. The fields on either side of Barton Lane had been excavated for gravel and infilled with household and industrial waste in the 1970s. They were later used for grazing ponies. Barton Lane continues down to the gravel pits and Thrupp.

The Science Park, known today as 'The Quadrant', is now a well-established business park. Leading computer anti-virus software company Sophos has established its world headquarters in Abingdon. Sophos is typical of the high-technology organisations which have been attracted to the town in recent years.

The Queen and Prince Philip are seen here entering the new Sophos building for its official opening in 2003. The building won an award in the major development category in a Design Award Scheme run by the Vale of White Horse District Council in 2006.

Above: An aerial photograph of Barton Court Farm c.1970. The cottage at one end of the large barn in the middle of the farmyard was formerly the farmhouse. A new farmhouse was built in the early 1930s beyond the large tree on the left.

The Audlett Drive housing estate was built on part of the farm land in the early 1980s. Audlett Drive, a new peripheral road incorporating part of Barton Lane, was named after John Audlett, the last Steward of Abingdon Abbey. The White Horse Leisure Centre, built in 2002 to replace the outdated facilities in Abingdon's Old Gaol, is just round the bend of the road on the right.

A painting of the house and farm buildings by John Barber. The farm lay behind the Warren Hospital and was occupied by the Benson family until it was demolished in 1974. The large old barn and cottage were taken down and are believed to have been re-erected on a site in Hampshire.

Rosemary and Ruth Benson on their way to school at Our Lady's Convent in the 1950s.

An early photograph of Thrupp Farmhouse at the end of Barton Lane, with a herd of young Aberdeen Angus cattle grazing nearby. The farmhouse was built on the Wick Hall estate in 1889 by Josephine Dockar Drysdale when she was developing the estate.

Thrupp is no longer a working farm as much of the surrounding land has been dug for gravel. The rich farmland which surrounded Abingdon, once so important to its status as a market town, has largely disappeared as the town has expanded. At one time there were nine dairy herds in the farms around Abingdon – now there are none.

Thrupp cottages, a pair of 17th century half-timbered cottages near Thrupp farmhouse. At one time this little hamlet had 16 inhabitants; another farmhouse and three more cottages stood on the south side of the branch railway line.

The cottages have been enlarged and modernised to make an attractive rural home.

David Homewood, one of John and Nancy Homewood's twin sons, on horseback at Peachcroft Farm in the 1970s. Peachcroft, which is owned by Radley College and farmed by the Homewood family, was a mixed farm of about 500 acres after the Second World War.

Around 100 acres of the farm land were sold for the Peachcroft housing estate in the 1970s. Since then the farm has developed a flourishing pick-your-own business as well as rearing turkeys and geese for the Christmas market. The former cottage (above) is now part of a farm shop and restaurant run by Wells Stores, selling a variety of home-made foods, specialist cheeses and produce from the farm. There is also a gift shop and a plant and shrub nursery.

9
Oxford Road to Northcourt

Cows from Mr James Candy's dairy herd graze in a field opposite Northcourt Farm, c.1939. The cows had names like Daisy, Buttercup and Bluebell. The fence marks the line of Monks Way, the old footpath from Northcourt to Sunningwell. The houses visible behind are in Picklers Hill and the field is now part of Shelley Close. The Candy Dairy was later to become a major business in Northcourt.

The old Roman Catholic Primary School (centre), now the church hall, seen from St. Edmund's Church, c.1930. The Oxford Road can be seen to the left with the Abingdon Workhouse, upper left. This was the first workhouse in the country to be built under the Poor Law Amendment Act of 1835. It was completed in six months at a cost of £8,500.

The workhouse was demolished in 1931 to build Abbot Road and Thesiger Road, then called the Oxford Road housing estate, part of which can be seen on the left.

Semi-detached houses on the Oxford Road on a wintry day in the 1920s. The Ox public house and the shops on the corner of St. John's Road have not yet been built, giving an open view to the backs of the houses in Swinburne Road.

The first shops to open here were a branch of Rant & Tombs grocers in 1927 and Thomas Leach newsagents in 1928, followed by Cottrell the butcher and Haycock's newsagents (later Mallows). The Ox public house just visible beyond was built in 1938 and a 'Laundromat' was added in the early 60s.

As well as the rebuilt laundry, now called a 'Launderette', the shops include IN-2 Motor Spares (formerly Abiparts), H D Tura's newsagents and grocery, and the Magic Wok Chinese Take-away.

The Boundary House seen here was built as a family home by Cyril Viney in 1922. Two of his grown-up children, Richard and Marie, are standing by the pond c.1948. The house was leased to Cecil Kimber, the Managing Director of the MG Car Company, from 1933 to 1938. It was then reoccupied by the Viney family. The house name commemorates the extension of the Borough boundary to Northcourt in 1892.

The Boundary House was acquired by the Morland Brewery and became a public house in 1962. Now owned by Greene King, it has been enlarged and extended over the years. The walnut tree on the left was planted by a member of the Viney family.

Two of Mr Candy's children, Michael and David, enjoy a walk through the fields with a family friend in 1939. The footpath led across the fields to Daisy Bank, a popular picnic spot. The Oxford Road is in the foreground with the Boundary House just out of sight on the right.

The rural scene above is now the busy junction of Northcourt Road and Oxford Road. The car park of the Boundary House can be seen on the right. The pine tree is one of two shown on the 1936 Ordnance Survey Map (see page 143).

The newly-built Rush Common House in Dorchester Crescent off Appleford Drive in 1960. This was a hostel built to accommodate mainly single young men who had come to work at the Atomic Energy Research Establishment (AERE) Harwell after the Second World War. The house just visible through the trees on the left is on the Oxford Road.

The hostel was demolished in the mid 1990s and replaced with a housing estate. The roads were named after the three major scientific research establishments in the area – Harwell Close, Culham Close and Rutherford Close. The Oxford Road house can be clearly seen.

A map of Northcourt in 1936. A row of bungalows and a few houses had been built along the Oxford Road, with four houses in what is now Picklers Hill, but the hamlet of Northcourt remained largely undeveloped at this date.

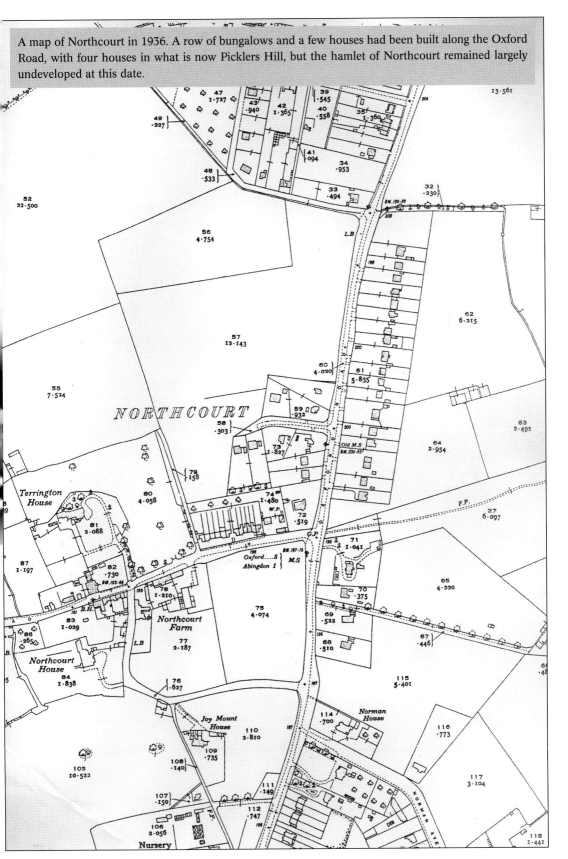

The Northcourt Tithe Barn seen from the farmyard in 1945. James Candy became tenant of Northcourt Farm in 1937. In 1946 he purchased the farm buildings and five acres of land from the Tatham family of Northcourt House. As the surrounding fields were lost to housing he stopped farming and built up the dairy business, putting in a small milk processing plant and collecting milk from local farms.

The beautifully restored Tithe Barn with Judy Thomas, one of the authors, in the foreground. The barn was bought by the Parish of Abingdon in 1960 and was converted into a place of worship, Christ Church, which opened in 1961. It now has one of the largest Anglican congregations in the Diocese of Oxford, including a sister congregation at Long Furlong.

The snow-covered farmyard, c.1939. On the left is the medieval bothy, with Northcourt Farmhouse (centre) and the milking parlour on the right.

The medieval bothy was built to house pigs, with the swineherd or farmhand living above.

By the 1970s the old bothy had become redundant and was replaced by an office building (left). The whole farm site apart from the farmhouse was acquired by Christ Church in 2001 for church and community use.

Philip Candy in the farm yard in 1946. Candy's milk float is on the right and there are milk churns outside the milking parlour.

James Candy with two of his four children, Philip and Jenny, and their cousin Jane Candy (right) outside the new Argyle & Candy dairy shop on Northcourt Road in 1958. The shop was created in the former bottling room and pasteurization plant. The dairy later became Elm Farm/Clifford Dairies, one of the largest dairy businesses in the UK.

A view of the old barns today. The dairy site was finally vacated in 1995. All the farm buildings now belong to Christ Church, and the former shop and milking parlour are occupied by the Abingdon Kindergarten.

Mr and Mrs John Loader outside 16 (now 22) Northcourt Road, c.1890. They brought up nine children in this cottage, which their family occupied for at least three generations. John (1845-1919) and one of his sons were gardeners to the Tatham family at Northcourt House. The blocked doorway shows that this was once two cottages. The Spread Eagle pub then occupied the next building on the right.

Six-year-old Joy Loader (Mrs Marriott) outside her home, no. 16 Northcourt Road, in 1930, with the Spread Eagle beyond. Joy and her sister Irma later married the twin Marriott brothers.

The Loaders' cottage, 22 Northcourt Road, is now part of the enlarged premises of the Spread Eagle pub. Formerly named the 'Eagle', the name and pub sign were changed to the 'Spread Eagle' during the First World War because of their resemblance to the German eagle. The gateposts of the Northcourt Centre can be seen beyond the wall on the left.

147

The Tatham Memorial Hall, c.1960. This ex-Army hut was built on land generously given by Miss Tatham, the owner of Northcourt House. It was used by two Women's Institutes, two Brownie packs, a clinic, and also for whist, bingo, wedding receptions and many other activities. Monthly services of Holy Communion were held here from 1955; following the appointment of the Rev. John Moore as Curate-in-charge in 1958, weekly Family Services and Evening Prayer were introduced, until Christ Church opened for worship in 1961.

The old hall was replaced by the present Northcourt Centre in 1969. It provides a venue for many organisations, including children's ballet classes, Scottish Country Dancing, the Abingdon Flower Club, the Horticultural Society and the Abingdon Area Archaeological & Historical Society. It is also used by the Fitzharris WI, the Peace Group and Weightwatchers, as a polling station and for Blood Donor sessions.

Northcourt House, the 'big house' of this small hamlet, in 1981. Built by Henry Knapp, an Abingdon banker, in 1805, the estate was bought by the Bowyer family in 1848 and became the dower house for Radley Hall. In 1902 it was bought by a Mr and Mrs Tatham who ran a 'crammer' there, coaching boys for examinations. Their daughter Sylvia and her sister later used the house as a preparatory school. Since Sylvia's death in 1975 the house has had several owners and was at one time part of Abingdon College of Further Education.

Northcourt House is once again a family home. The classical proportions of this elegant mansion form a perfect cube.

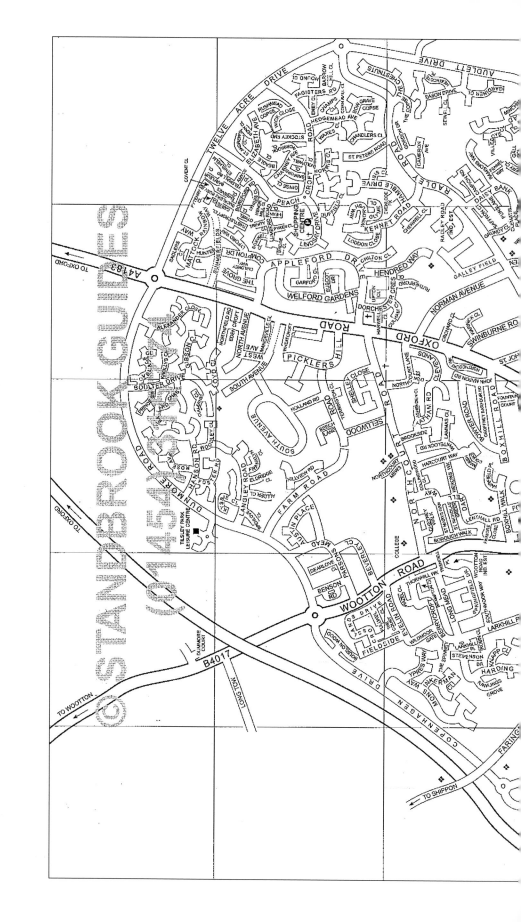

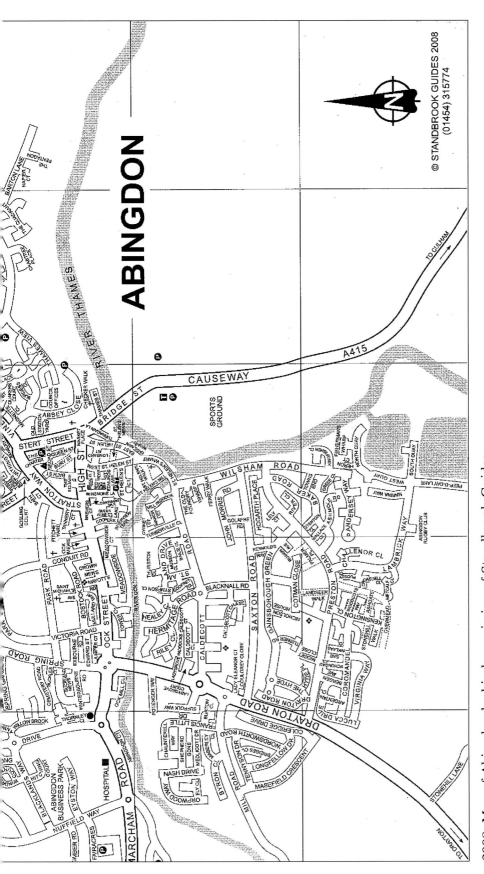

2008 Map of Abingdon by kind permission of Standbrook Guides

ACKNOWLEDGMENTS

The authors wish to extend heartfelt thanks to the following organisations and individuals who have so generously contributed images and information to make this book possible: The curator and staff of Abingdon Museum, the staff of Oxfordshire Studies Department, National Monuments Record, Abingdon Area Archaeological & Historical Society, Abingdon Conservative Club, Abingdon School, Aero Pictorial Ltd., Carswell School, Friends of Abingdon, Newsquest, Nuffield Press Ltd., Sophos plc, Standbrook Guides, UKAEA Harwell, Les Argyle, Pauline Bagg, David Banfield, Mrs Barber, Michael Bellinger, Ruth Binning (nee Benson), Philip Candy, Brian Clark, Viola Crowe (nee Viney), Charles Dockar-Drysdale, Patrick Dockar-Drysdale, John Enock, Ivor Fields, Simon Fletcher, Andy Greenaway, David Gully, Roy Hallett, Nigel Hammond, Walter Harland, Jim Hayden, Edna Hole, Nancy Homewood, Beryl Horne, Jackie Hudson, Godfrey Jones, Heather Law, Jonathan Leach, Irma Marriott, Bill Mellor, C. Milligan, Rev. John Moore, Brian Moylan, John Reed, Alan Rowe, Pat Russell, Connie Silvester, Doug Small, Jacqueline Smith, Mrs Anne Spokes-Symonds, Derek Steptoe, Colin Wiggins.

We are especially grateful to Mieneke Cox, Jacqueline Smith and Roger Thomas for reviewing the text and pictures and sharing their knowledge and expertise; to Edward, James, Sam and William Drury for their technical help, and to our husbands, Spencer White and Alan Drury, for their ongoing support and encouragement.

Every attempt has been made to contact the copyright holders of the images in this book. We apologise for any omissions in our acknowledgments.

The last train on the Abingdon branch railway line prepares to leave for Oxford with the Mayor on board in June 1984. Regular passenger services had been withdrawn under the Beeching cuts in 1963, but the line remained viable with coal trains and regular car transporter wagons carrying MG cars, until the MG factory closed in 1980. Waitrose supermarket now occupies the site.